Contents

The recycling centre

A **recycling** centre is where **recyclable** materials are sorted and stored. This recycling centre has a **drop-off site** and a **depot** where materials are taken for recycling. Some materials are collected as part of a box scheme.

People drive their cars or vans to the drop-off site to unload their recycling. The site workers help people to unload.

Each material is sorted into a separate container.

Big trucks are used to take the containers of materials to other sites or factories to be recycled.

Collecting boxes

Each home in this street has a box to fill with recyclable materials and put out for collection. Then the collectors sort the materials into a truck.

The teams

The recycling centre team do lots of different jobs, such as driving trucks, operating machinery, and sorting materials.

This team work at the drop-off site. They work together to sort and transport the recyclables.

Karl is the **supervisor** at the drop-off site. He uses a **walkie-talkie** to keep in touch with the rest of the team.

Paul (right) is the **manager** of the recycling centre. Here, he is talking to Chris, a site worker, about some changes he is planning to make at the depot.

Diane works in the depot office.

This team travel by truck from home to home collecting boxes of recyclables.

Starting the day

The recycling centre opens early in the morning.

Jim is a truck driver. He signs his **timesheet** at the drop-off site office.

Then Jim checks his truck and makes sure he has a full tank of fuel.

Paul puts on his **high-visibility** jacket in the **locker** room. All the site workers wear brightly-coloured safety clothes. This is so they can be seen clearly as they work on a busy site.

'I wear a bright jacket so I can be seen by all the vehicles.'
Paul, site worker

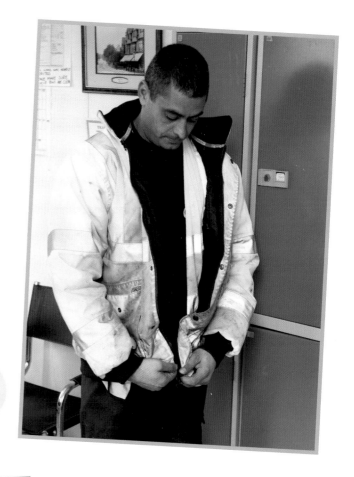

Karl unlocks the gates so people can drive their cars and vans in and out of the site.

Cars start to arrive. People drive in to drop off their materials for recycling.

The drop-off site

The drop-off site is for household materials and waste only. One of the site workers stays by the gate to check what people are dropping off. The striped barrier above the gate stops people driving big vans in.

'Sometimes there are long queues of cars waiting to drive in.'
Karl, site supervisor

Karl is taking a **booking** on the phone. Big vans have to be booked in to arrive at a certain time so the barrier can be lifted.

Karl stores information on a **database** about the materials that are collected from and transported to the different sites.

Recycled waste

The **green waste** that is collected at the site is taken away to be recycled into **compost**. The bags of compost are then brought back to the recycling centre and sold to people visiting the site.

Paul helps customers to load the bags of compost into their cars.

Unloading recycling

Cars and vans are driven in to the drop-off site so the different materials can be unloaded into the containers.

The site workers keep the site clean and tidy. Paul sweeps up any materials that are dropped on the ground as people unload.

There is a row of big containers for materials such as metal, green waste and wood.

The site workers check what each person is dropping off, and show them where to park and unload materials.

As the containers get fuller, the digger is used to crush the materials to make more room.

Different materials

Each area or container is labelled so that people know where to put the different materials. Paper is posted into a special 'paper bank'.

Each material is sorted so it can be loaded on to a truck and taken to a different site to be recycled.

The wood container is next to the cardboard one. The wood is recycled by cutting it in to small pieces to make **chipboard**.

The metals are recycled by being melted down and used again.

The cardboard is recycled to make new cardboard **packaging**.

Recycling fridges and freezers

Fridges and freezers need to be specially recycled. They contain dangerous parts that need to be taken apart carefully, and only some parts can be recycled.

The box scheme

On the box scheme, the recycling collectors drive round from street to street. They collect and empty all the boxes of recycling into their truck.

Lamin sorts the materials before he carries the boxes to the truck.

The collectors sort the materials into different sections of their truck. Chris sorts a box of tins and bottles into the right containers.

Abrahim (left) tips a load of newspapers into the paper container.

'It's less messy for us if people wash out their cans and bottles.'
Abrahim, recycling collector

Boxes of materials

In each area, every household is given a box. Glass bottles and jars, newspapers, magazines and other materials can be put out for recycling.

Unloading trucks

Once the collection trucks have finished their rounds, they drive back to the depot. The driver unlocks the **safety bars**, so the containers can be unloaded.

Each driver empties out the metal cans container first. Gary pulls the cans out with a rake and adds them to a huge pile.

Then Chris uses a **fork-lift truck** to unload the containers. He empties each container full of materials on to the right pile.

Recycling cans

These cans are made from metals called aluminium and steel. The different metals can be separated and melted down to make more cans or other things such as parts for machines.

Moving materials

Once a container of materials is full, it is lifted out and transported by truck to another site. Jim **reverses** his truck up to the container.

Then Jim uses **lifting gear** to load the container on to the back of the truck.

After the container is loaded on, Jim drives on to a **weighbridge** to check the load is not too heavy.

Jim picks up a **weigh bill**. Then he is ready to set off to deliver the container.

Keeping records

The recycling centre keeps records of all the materials that are collected and transported. When Jim gets back from a delivery, he gives the weigh bill to Karl in the office.

Recycling metals

The metals are taken to a scrap metal yard to be recycled. The container is opened up by the driver. Then it is tipped up and emptied. All the different metals will be sorted and separated for recycling.

The metals are sorted into piles by big machines. This crane has a big grabbing claw to pick up the metals and move them into one pile.

This crane (left) uses a huge **magnet** to sort the metals into different types, and to move them around.

'It's interesting to think that an aluminium can may be reused to make part of a plane.'
Jim, truck driver

Metal blocks

Metals of the same type are squashed into big blocks. These blocks are taken to factories to be melted down and used again.

Recycling glass and paper

Huge lorries drive into the depot to collect the materials to take to recycling factories.

Mick uses the digger to load glass into the lorry.

Afterwards Mick and Chris sweep up any glass that has fallen on the ground.

The glass is recycled by being broken into small pieces and melted down to be used again in new bottles and jars.

Loads of paper are scooped up by the digger and dropped into the lorry. Once the lorry is full, the driver sets off to take the paper to the **newsprint** factory.

Recycling paper

At the newsprint factory, the paper is chopped into pieces and hot water is added to make a mushy **pulp**. The pulp is cleaned, squashed, dried and pressed to make new sheets of paper.

At the landfill site

Household rubbish is collected at the drop-off site but cannot be recycled. The rubbish is taken to a **landfill site**.

Jim drives the truck into the landfill site. Then he opens the back of the container and tips out the rubbish.

Big machines squash the rubbish down, and then bury it with a layer of soil.

Reducing rubbish

One day we are going to run out of room to bury our rubbish in landfill sites like these. It is important to reduce the waste that we send to the landfill site and to recycle as much as we can.

The end of the day

At the end of the day, Jim takes a disk out of a machine in the truck. This machine has made a record of all his journeys for the day.

All the information about times and distances is printed on disks of paper like this.

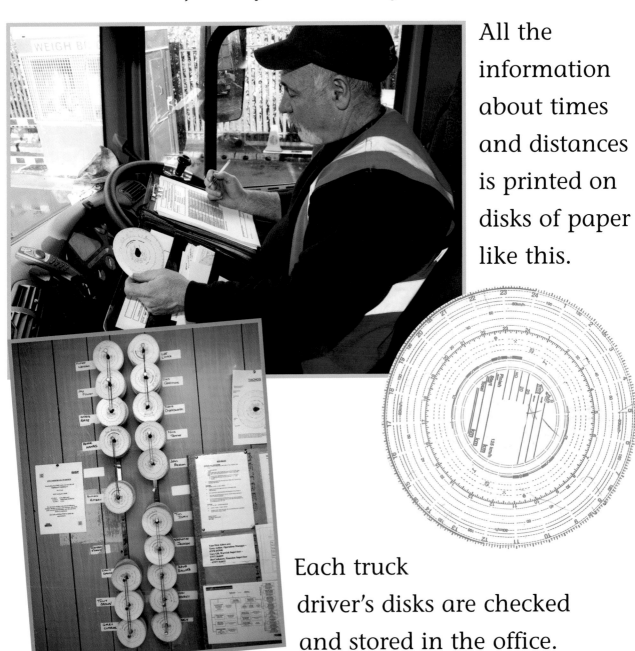

Each truck driver's disks are checked and stored in the office.

At closing time, no more cars are allowed in. Then, once the last car has driven out of the exit, Karl closes and locks the gates.

The site workers put their work clothes in their lockers. The site buildings are locked up, and it's time to go home.

Glossary

booking a particular time and place to go to do something.

chipboard board made by pressing pieces of wood and glue together.

compost material used for growing plants.

database a computer program used to store information.

depot buildings and yards where materials or machinery are stored.

drop-off site a site where things can be unloaded and stored.

fork-lift truck a vehicle used for unloading containers. It has two metal parts on the front that can be used to lift containers.

green waste garden waste such as leaves, hedge trimmings or grass clippings that will rot down.

high-visibility something that is made to be seen clearly.

landfill site a huge hole in the ground where rubbish is buried.

lifting gear machinery used to lift things.

locker a cupboard used for storing coats and other belongings.

magnet a piece of iron or steel that attracts other pieces of iron and steel.

manager someone who is in charge of a place of work.

newsprint a type of paper that is used to print newspapers.

packaging the container you buy something in.

pulp a soft mixture like porridge.

recyclable able to be recycled.

recycling using something again or making it into something else.

reverses go backwards.

safety bars strong metal strips used to keep something closed.

supervisor someone who is in charge of a team of workers.

timesheet a piece of paper to write down times worked.

walkie-talkie a wireless radio for sending and receiving messages.

weigh bill a piece of paper that shows how much something weighs.

weighbridge a big machine that trucks can drive on to so they can be weighed.

Further information

Websites

www.recyclezone.org.uk Plenty of information and activities on reducing and reusing rubbish.

www.glassforever.co.uk Full of facts about glass packaging and recycling.

www.thinkcans.net All you need to know about recycling cans.

www.collect4school.co.uk A good site for finding out about recycling at school.

www.recycle-more.co.uk Lots of information, including a bank locator to help you find out about recycling facilities in your area.

Books

Reusing and Recycling (series of 6 books), Ruth Thomson, Franklin Watts, 2006

Recycling Materials (Making A Difference series), Sue Barraclough, Franklin Watts, 2006

Recycle our Rubbish (I Can Help series), Viv Smith, Franklin Watts, 2001

Index